UEA POETRY 2016

UNIVERSITY OF EAST ANGLIA
CREATIVE WRITING MA
POETRY ANTHOLOGY 2016

INTRODUCTION

TIFFANY ATKINSON

'PEOPLE USE LANGUAGE for two reasons,' writes poet and critic Dean Young, 'to be understood and not to be understood.'[1] But poetry is the third reason, the art form that kicks up the terrain between these poles most assiduously, most insightfully and most playfully. Poetry makes energetic use of the tensions between lucidity and bafflement, what may and may not be said, convention and revolution, and any other pragmatic binary. It is language having it both ways: indeed, it is language, potentially, having it every which way.

So it is perhaps a limit on ambition for a poet to identify his or her work with one or other philosophy of language-use – 'lyric' or 'experimental,' et cetera – as though language may only do one thing at a time; as though each poem were not in itself a fresh assertion of linguistic possibility and a kicking over of the last generation's traces. Happily, the poets introduced in this anthology are less concerned with staking out positions than with getting their hands dirty/bitten/ecstatic in the effort to break habituated ways of reaching for and into the world through their poetry. Thus it is much to their credit that they have little in common beyond this wild and never-more-timely ambition, and the dedicated, sometimes frustrating, often hilarious, genuinely rather mysterious hours spent in each other's company, bringing it to fruition. Long may the discoveries continue.

Al Anderson's poetry in particular makes varied assaults on the expectations of lyric poetry. Shifts of voice, perspective and form, and elements of aesthetic and linguistic philosophy collide with the ever-delayed promise of sincerity. The results are both witty and poignant: in 'a rabbit considers the limits of desire,' '[t]he rabbit decides to / stop regarding himself / in the third person. // "quit it" / he says / "quit it" / he says ' / "quit it."'

1. Dean Young, *The Art of Recklessness: Poetry as Assertive Force and Contradiction* (Minneapolis: Graywolf Press, 2010) p.38.

In Meghann Boltz's troubling interrogations of gendered and consumerist iconography, language is plastic in every sense, glossy with artifice and malleable under pressure, lending her poems an utterly contemporary irony: 'if there is an angel to SAVE / US she will be *sleek, silver & / streamlined* with a COLTAN soul. / girl.' She is also a bold and protean experimenter with voice: 'i went to see the wizard & asked him for a cock,' says one such narrator: 'he must have / seen by the scuffs on my knees that I really / needed one because he said ok.'

Eleanor Chandler's poems bring an unflinching global and environmental awareness to bear on the absurdity and creeping menace of everyday capitalism. A riff on international varieties of KitKats leads to a meditation on consumerist logic; a Japanese language-learner finds in the slippages of translation an inadvertent expression of an essentially poetic struggle: 'if there are no sounds beyond herself / some verbs cannot be used for outward transfer.'

The prose poem may function as a compressed container in which language and thoughts can circle and mutate, and Georgia Hingston's poems are tightly pressurised and transformative containers, breaching the membrane between real and fictional or mythic worlds to both comic and unsettling, but always intensely sensory, effect: 'it is always autumn – eating salt – chocolate / yields between the teeth with a satisfying clunk. / The year is the colour of merlot.'

Of course a poem's 'voice' is never singular but contains multitudes. Joanna Hollins's poetic avatar *ES* (electro sapiens) flickers through her poems and 'gives as good as she's / given gives as good as / god gave her gives her / grandmother reason / to complain she's got / a lonely pinkflushed / piercing;' a tonal dexterity through which Joanna also invigorates the traditional form of the sonnet, making it fresh and elastic.

Sean Wai Keung's poetry dispenses with tired distinctions between work for 'page' and 'stage,' having a kinetic, three-dimensional quality that brings the wit, timing and rhythms of live performance onto the page, while also swooping effortlessly from daily vicissitudes into unexpected territory: 'I have yet to figure out how best to structure / each of my prayers into language,' concludes the speaker of a poem called, pragmatically, 'I am on the floor cutting roast duck into bits.'

Keely Laufer's poems work by the accretion and compaction of image and syntax to create their own startling metaphorical logic, often throwing new light on matters of cultural displacement, embarrassment and intimacy. A French horn on an off-day becomes 'potato-tongued / with a potato hand in her mouth she' s got to / sing through, the potato in the room / we seem to hide in our mouths.' Elsewhere, a student at a Russian-learners' cultural event, in a paroxysm of disorientation, 'eat[s] each flake of embarrassment / off of the face of the sun.'

'The Practical Application of Ionospherics,' by Elizabeth Lewis Williams, draws inventively on the visual potential of page space to create a dynamic poetic of the archive; a space in which the hazards of radio transmission to the Antarctic, 'coax[ing] / a signal from the needle's flicker' may also bring forth unbidden the mysterious 'songs of auroral space' – almost a metaphor for the animating tensions of poetry itself.

Rosie Quattromini's poems are full of different, Cartesian struggles, where moments of lyric intensity tug almost erotically against philosophical rigour: 'st ambrose was the first person / to read without moving his lips / but still he followed the words / with his finger; flesh against ink / on paper.' Despite the difficulty in articulating 'what i really want to say,' nowhere more acute than in her elegiac 'essay' for the late Jenny Diski, Rosie's poetry asserts, in the end, the pragmatic optimism of the will to write: 'it is like this, and this is what we do.'

Tiffany Atkinson, *convenor of the MA in Creative Writing: Poetry*

AL ANDERSON

LAST NIGHT MY BLOOD
FLOWED BACKWARDS

the adolescent mechanism is powered by three muscles
     oil & gas & liquid pumps
   awkward cogs rolling through the street to the party
          alone
the smell of cold must mean something
   'always open with a lie, that way you're invincible'
the look, glazed look, manic look, half shut, glutted on
          sleep,
       bullshit rumbling out of it like tomorrow's not coming
   Jean Genet & Joni Mitchell & other imaginary friends
it dreams a perfect face either its own or touching its own
          it thinks it's in love with you   let it ruin you
it's   the quintessence of teenage cupidity
: self hatred and perfect narcissism
their form warped beneath synthetic light
                  feeling tragically / beautifully / ugly / perfect

       homosex is affect only, like Rimbaud & putting make-
          up on in secret
 – in the spirit of hostility smash up a phone box on the way
          home –
rehearse this one in the bathroom   mirror then over the
          toilet bowl
   I got us lost on purpose because
       I wanted the feeling of being lost with you
   I say I love you to myself but don't really buy it
& I'll say it   to you one day & you'll look at me like I'm
          a faggot
which is what I'll have been all along & all these words
       just faggot's words, weak & desperate to impress
  pumped out of my faggot heart
       bitter autumn cold taking ride in your bones scraping
          your eyes

loose your grip on the fuck rot red wine haze white wine
    hangover screaming
  you are, what I mean is,
        you know what are, no, what I mean is, you are, I
      mean, you are

A RABBIT CONSIDERS THE
LIMITS OF DESIRE

'I need to stop taking drugs' says the rabbit.
'That's just the drugs talking' says a boy in a mint scarf and
        pink beret.

                    *

A fan oscillates so slowly it almost doesn't exist at all.
The rabbit smokes a cigarette and contemplates the waning
        ubiquity of neon.
He says 'don't' as the boy puts a finger to his cleft.

The boy tells the rabbit where he is from, what it was like
        growing up, how his mother consulted three differ-
        ent child psychologists after she found him wearing
        flowers in his hair.

'Boys with flowers in their hair are beautiful things,'
says the rabbit, typically slow, typically affected,
'they deserve to be punished.'

The boy gets up and walks across the room,
in the perfection of his buttocks
the rabbit recognises some sense of redemption.

He picks an apple core from the waste paper basket, says
        'poetry as this.'

'I guess'
says the rabbit
watching
the sweat & the dust
coalesce in the
6:00pm sun

*

The rabbit decides to
stop regarding himself
in the third person

'quit it'
he says
'quit it'
he says
'quit it'

VARIATIONS ON A SEA
OF INDIFFERENCE

– every sentence is considered, despised, written down anyway – for six months you carry a letter around in your pocket informing you that you've been issued a £200 fine – this is your albatross – you overhear three different conversations, from three different people, in the same café, about the novels started but never completed – your fingers sticky with ice-cream, you are feeling agonisingly Anglo-Saxon – you have a long conversation with a friend about depression as critical enquiry, he tells you depression is something that must be harnessed to create something 'beautiful', he says this is the basis of his latest film. three months later you see his film and it's terrible. – you are Kafka, you die in the June of 1924, leaving *The Castle* unfinished – you feel so happy you could vomit – you drink three cartons of sugared almond milk and throw up sweet baby sick over your lover's shoulder – you drown yourself in the sea but don't drown – you consider the confessional lyric, you don't – in your sleep you meet Mayakovsky, he says 'I don't care for you.' – a fox comes into your garden during the daytime – you hear a friend from years ago has been sectioned, you say 'oh' – you go from poet to conceptual writer to avant-gardist to your first serious suicide attempt – you watch hours of interviews with Werner Herzog on YouTube – you count all the planes that fly over your house – you consider the obscenity of all love poetry – 'oh', 'oh', 'oh', 'oh', – you're reading Marguerite Duras on the South Bank at sunset – you consider the obscenity of all poetry – you live in a folder on the computer called 'unfinished'. it grows every day. – 54 – you have an 8-hour conversation with your echo – you pay homage to Antonin Artaud with a psychotic episode, cutting off all your toes – you are 15 or 16, you meet a boy called Henri in

10 Belles, Paris. you lose his phone number   –   you curse
modernism and all it has wrought   –   you are in love,
through the hole in his shirt you can see the sky   –   a
horse breathes on the window, it is white, then brown, it is
maybe a dream   –

WE GO TO THE GALLERY

without flesh or warmth,
but with these things

implied in the same way
smoke from far away implies

a person

the act of remembering
is the same as
looking at a painting

you're not looking at something that
is about something else, you're looking
at an original:

like 'I' look at 'you'
standing in the doorway
wearing a towel
trying to find
the outline of
your cock
because I
know it's there

like 'you' show 'me'
a photo of you at 15
& tell me it was taken
the night you lost your virginity
& I think about it
for

        weeks & weeks & weeks

trying to trace the outline
of you, then
with the wholeness
of you, now

if you touch it
during the drying process
the mark will be there forever

you lend me money for a
pack of cigarettes & buy a
can of Tyskie that we share

& all I can do
is look at you

trying to void
all thoughts of

the boy

taking off
his clothes,

strapping on his toy wings
which chafe his smooth back

posing as
love

I wonder if he was
made to feel at ease
was offered
buttered artichoke hearts
had the quiet beauty
of his collar bones
commented upon

if he
stumbled
getting
into position

suddenly aware
of how naked
he was

& said

sorry, sorry, sorry

MEGHANN BOLTZ

CHOMP STOMP

Louche-lipped Looney Tune, do not pass GO

One minute I'm Joan of Arc, the next
you're burning me at the stake

Some babies are just born before others

We all know nothing
lasts forever
      not bubbles & not
      boys   Quick –

find a way to make it painful so
it's bearable, then collect $200

        [hope
        ages
        fast]

Shoe to the St Charles, driver plays
death metal (dreamworld)
        mean while

this gum has lost its *joie de vivre*

You can outlast anything – even
love – just always remember

        to brush your teeth.

I ♥ IT HERE

SILLY GIRL go *swing* your
ponytail somewhere else girl girl
the *bottom line* is always RIGHT
below your BELLY button slip this
speculum inside stick-on lips hand
me the petroleum   jelly hit
delete: rinse, repeat get on TV
girl

> fake palm trees look
> realer than real palm
> trees which look
> fake under studio
> lights

exude the illusion you exist we'll
put you on meat hooks & pretend to
cry when you die just LOVE ME or
leave me but love me a little t&a or
EST if there is an angel to SAVE
US she will be *sleek, silver* &
streamlined with a COLTAN soul.
girl.

BUCK

i went to see the wizard & asked him for a cock   he
must have seen by the scuffs on my knees that i really
needed one because he said ok i buy a 3-pack of white
hanes classic men's undershirts a pair of 501 original
fit levi's and a carton of marlboro reds to fit snug in
the roll of my sleeve then i try *it* out swinging it around
it makes a nice lasso & i find i can use it to catch the
pretty girls in town when i pull them in close enough
for a kiss they rub rigid against the taut crotch of my
new jeans one girl says but i don't even know your
name i tell her to call me Buck and i lead her back to
my place in the naked overhead light of the bedroom
her brown hair turns mousy & her bare ass is dimpled
with cellulite but her nipples are hard so i light one of
the reds then close my eyes as she reaches inside my
jeans & i think about how good this feels

SUPERSTAR

I'm going to pump [   ] full of laxatives
Karen Carpenter.

Nothing ever seems to fit [   ]
Karen Carpenter.

[   ] not in control any more
Karen Carpenter.

Don't roll [   ] eyes at me
Karen Carpenter.

Oh, [   ] such a phony
Karen Carpenter.

I hate [   ]
Karen Carpenter.

[   ]
Karen Carpenter.

Karen Carpenter.

Karen.

Kare.

Kar.

Ka.

K.

.

STFU

the tower of ba-
bel has crashed in
the alien corn & i,
pitiful   illusion
ruth,   lay   pros-
trate   under   dog
o, but this is the
wreckage   that's
better than (o'hara
under now, leaves)
no one
~~venus~~ aphrodite
is going to dig
uranus's
castration out i'll
be   sea   foam   of
pompeii   gar-
gling up the blood
tinged *forgive me*
these   allusions
looking   on   in
disdain   i've
been
i   blame   my
dumbness on the
fact that i may
have   suffered
(most)
immeasurably   &
the   this   great
babbling
infrastructure   has
jubileed my
r   u   b   b   l   e

INSUFFICIENT FUNDS

this time i didn't try
to buy you
an island

              well,
              i did,

but my credit card
was de-

clined & when i
didn't try again

              i knew i wasn't

in
lovewithyou

              any more.

ELEANOR CHANDLER

CONTINUOUS LINE DRAWINGS

if I have a spoonful of cuttlefish
if I catch the thin leaf of a telephone call
if the pipette is both round and long
how do I count it?

> *I could be counting bowls of rice or*
> *puffs of a cigarette*

if a photograph of a car is printed
on a piece of paper inside a thick encyclopedia
what is heavy?

if I chop very much
of the coriander why does the tomato
sauce come in buckets rather than syringes?

if my tongue comes back negative
if I lay a wreath on the grave of my laptop
do crime scenes ever become empty?

what if following
shadows is an obsolete way of telling
the time?

> *other properties may be measured*
> *according to the angle of my wrist or*
> *the number of insects within my gait*

if rabbit ears are unusable wings of an extinct bird
if futuristic white buildings are cakes of tofu

all I need are
guns, sticks of ink, violins

> *but this does not look like any*
> *other shape I've ever met*

LOVELY WOMAN (N.)

with the connotation of not being
streetwise

having been invited
she unfolds into the present
sound

she is caught
sound   she
        gnaws through
with muscular embouchure
the bell under her splaying
mellow

oil shock
it is an oil shock out there

this pattern
ruin to the extent that she might
then   there's the question
the entire excursion of
persimmon more
than oyster rather
than fence
the order and arrangement of boxes

to go	(into) sotto voce
to be	plosive
to exhale	hard
	in the face of a complete stranger
to attack	(describing waves breaking on the shore)

if there are no sounds beyond herself
some verbs cannot be used for outward transfer

YOU WILL SURELY WIN

Kit Kat is Japan's #1 selling chocolate bar.

      I can buy a blue cheese flavoured Kit Kat.
              a cherry blossom flavoured Kit Kat.
              a gold leaf-covered Kit Kat.
              a purple potato flavoured Kit Kat.
              a grape Kit Kat.
              a French Rock Salt Kit Kat.
                watermelon
                Hokkaido roasted corn
                cider and pepper
                soy sauce

      I can buy a green tea flavoured Kit Kat.

This is a special
type of powdered
green tea
      used in a traditional tea ceremony. It is performed by
geishas in tatami rooms.
They sit on their knees.
It is a scene of Zen and Serenity and Meditation. There is
      a lot of bowing.

I bring the cup to my face
      and drink the tea
         in three
         mouthfuls:
      it is thick, strong and foamy. I leave feeling cleansed.

In the early eighteenth century, Christopher (Kit) Katt's London pub served mutton pies, often dubbed 'Kit-Kats'. A group of white men regularly met at the pub to eat pies and drink beer and discuss resistance to France and the Protestant succession to the throne. Members included Sir Robert Walpole and John Locke. The chocolate covered wafer bar was invented in York in the 1930s to provide a snack for men to take to work.

Pronounced kitto katto
Kit Kat is very similar to the phrase きっと勝つ

> lit. you will surely win
> or I hope you do well
> or good luck

Understanding the culture and the context in which services and products are consumed helps companies be more successful when crossing borders. Understanding how to consume more companies and products when crossing borders helps contextualise culture. Consumption of cultures helps products be more successful. Cross-consuming more products and services *is* understanding culture and context. Crossing cultures consumes more success. Companies understand that successful borders help consumption.

It tastes bitter and sweet and good.

GEORGIA HINGSTON

CACTI

Arizona is the only state in America where
saguaros grow. Tall but unassuming, gangly
residents of the Sonoran desert. At night the
air smells a curious combination of star anise
and over-ripe melon. You become such a lover
of colours no one knew were in existence you
forget the bright armoured bugs skittering over
your feet, a wonder of wing-casing and slender
legs, the dart of tawny mice scuttling in tun-
nels below your soles, and other less innocuous
beasts.

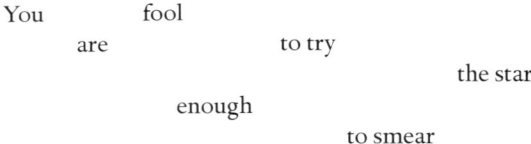

You   fool
        are   to try
                                        the stars
                enough
                        to smear
                                        with

grubby fingers   certain they could recite some-
thing hidden in a hummingbird's heartrate.
Head back   mouth wide
convinced you will swallow something of the
deepest purple-red mountains. Tracking the
moon while headlights beetle distant through
the darkness   flick over the horizon.
    You linger   hair growing stiff as spikelets of
witchgrass   burrow your feet into
the sand. When the
sun comes up you stand   holding small white
flowers with cream yellow centres that close
against the heat   a home for the hollows   of
gilded flickers   tiny wide-eyed elf owls.

THE BENDS

*

I am a vacuum sealed ration
kept fresh in an airtight packet
*

There is no sound in a perfect

                                               there is no sound
                                               there is no sound
                                               there is no

dust for fingerprints in a vacuum
in a belljar where
tea and news are
beamed in accordingly
*
*

decompress
*
*

my pushed buttons
I don't want my buttons pressed
it is no longer fun
*
*
*

decompress my cabin in
a vibrant location
re-inflate me
reduce the air pressure but
bring me up slowly
*
*
*

use patience to
avoid paralysis

and nausea
especially when building
underwater
*

*

*

*

slowly approach the surface
as a blue whale
even though it's miles below
it's possible to
hear whalesong so
come
up
slowly
*

*

*

*

decompress me
*

*

*

*

if you will
go down
*

*

*

*

*

on my foundations
come up slowly
slowly slowly
*

*

*
*
*
listen
for whalesong
but remember

                                        there is no sound
                                        there is no sound
                                        there is

CAISSON

iron bell wooden boxed be decompressed lest
nitrogen behave an aero in an inside pocket
chocolate blood incapacitated tiny digging dirt
from the bed dirt in the gloom dig in the blood
truffle in my room take skin grafts to send to the
surface till hit bone fill cavities with concrete
better knock are honeycomb holes full of
oxygen how hot must they get to liquidate and
lose their shape do not think of weight of water
eardrums can seep their own song of sorrow
draw me up rush me pull up slowly decompress
me push me up paralytic at the site of the sun.

TAROT

People feel you look feel more than see through
glass or intuition a depth level a weight on a crab
cable – butterflies only live a maximum of two
days – like fork lighting or glow worms there are
gestures the place where the hook slides – *right
behind the eyes* – bone and locket ball and socket
an alignment an escarpment of trees an old man
and endless October rain. Not to be confused
with observation,
      ticks tart as a blurted declaration,
flaked pages bent corners better loved than
strangers at stations accents that stir the smell
of kanel and an extra roll on the waist pliant and
ripe as bread dough in that other place from
spoons of honey in your coffee.

*

It is always autumn – eating salt – chocolate
yields between the teeth with a satisfying clunk.
The year the colour of merlot. *Did you know
people take longer showers when they live alone?*
And there's a high-pitched whistle through the
cables today so bury your tongue hold your
cramping abdomen whisper and soothe them
for they are easier to calm than other parts,
      recommendation:
go running in the rain drink builder's tea and
listen to pop with a solid back beat.

*

It is easy, said the woman on the corner, *it is
easy*, all bangles livered hands and turquoise

shawls –

it is easy
to sleep and never put hand to paper or key –
would you ever let anyone, even she.

AT THE MOVIES:
'LAST STAGE TO RED ROCK'
AFTER TARANTINO'S
'THE HATEFUL EIGHT'

Frontier justice is in us split across two sets of seats made sceptical by low lighting and the smell of popcorn. Do we have that much blood between us? Laughing at a nose breaking blow. Left with various sizes of fat lip, feet flat to gummy lino. Surveying beatings and bleedings in clouds of coffee, falling snow.

An arm rests, radioactive, shift of shoulders in conditioned darkness, pinned at the periphery. Messages into silence. A smile, a translucent bell of fluorescing blue.

Mouths lift and form pupils wide with expectation, dry cough, a tilt of the chin, sip of coke to clear the throat.

Be nonchalant: an exhalation of hot breath, slam of rifle-butt to chest, the crossing, recrossing of legs.

JOANNA HOLLINS

(I) ELECTRO-SAPIEN BLUES

:

electro-electro-electro

:

her dutch technique
her voxpopping hips
her jaguar gentleness

:

yes, electro-sapiens is
a good kid, your mum
's favourite, thanks her
for sweets says nothing
at the muffled sound
of your parents fighting

:

gives as good as she's
given gives as good as
god gave her gives her
grandmother reason
to complain she's got
a lonely pinkflushed
piercing

:

digikid with her own
hi-fi stereo and head-
phones paid in part
by kissing Charlie B
he's given her his heart
on MSN

:

she's a gen y thing all

salt no vinegar Avril
Lavigne except she's
not really a singer

       :

       :

all film no trailer
all ship no sailor

       :

kisses the future it's
a sliproad : she
is E.S. and yes

       :

lovely-electric-alive

(II) E.S. BY HER CO-ORDINATES

Latitude: E.S. is North
of her mother & the circle
drawn to protect her

the degree is 52°3'11 so
the age of her father
in decimal and the age

of her doubts
in dog years

*

Longitude: her friends
have been searching
for her for hours

E.S. is not picking up
E.S. is following the sun

& the sun is making an exit West

so she's moving too,
0°49'14
0°49'13

(III) E.S. IS WRITING

E.S. is writing found poetry she writes
this is a poem from voices on the underground:
      (I was in the carriage I heard everything)

E.S. is writing found poetry she writes
this is a poem from titles of poems about transport:
      (I heard this voice on the underground)

E.S. is writing found poetry she writes
this is a poem from poems about hectic modern living:
      (I heard so many poems about living
       I heard so many poems about moving)

E.S. is writing found poetry she writes
this is a poem from poems about now & modern life
      (I heard how hectic modern life is
       I heard this voice on the underground
       It was saying it was saying)

E.S. is writing found poetry she writes
this is a poem about poems this is the teleology of poems
      (I heard this is where they came from
       I heard the voice on the underground saying
       so many poems up for the finding)

E.S. is writing
      (and before god and before god and before god
                 nothing)

WHERE EDEN

Where eden is
there are teenagers reminiscing
and park gates bound up
by silly string &
the flat impresses of yesterday's
flowers

in each other's pockets
we're dreaming weeks
of each other, yes to tender
nights outside
and heavens after

all of the quizmasters
have better teams
than us

all of the girls waiting
round eden's park railings
buttercup under cheeks
give you lips

ripe
for your
picking

OF ME & YOU & MYSELF

So it's just me in for the night, the TV
tuned to the radio, blank blue screen,

dishes piling up in the sink, silence
bar the distant gurgle of the drain.

The static hum of you is growing loud.
I'm punch-drunk happy, or at least think so.

Six drink me is talking in my head. Go out,
she says, be careless while you're young.

Between us she makes the room a crowd
and in my mind you are arguing too. The radio

is all but drowned out. I kill the lights
and end up week-night punch-drunk sad

in for the night with the TV beaming blue
disappointing her and disappointing you.

THE LORD GOD AND SON,
FAMILY BUILDERS

On the site, God
rolls a steel joist against his palms
cracks knuckles 1 to 8
adjusts the sun like a reading light

& sets to sawing & general carpentry
(he was originally a plumber
but landwork's crept up on him)

Today's project: number thirty-seven
& the uneven foundation repair
on their conservatory, tomorrow

scaffolding (Skegness, 1.30)
round the faith
of an elderly Catholic priest
who God swears calls him out

more for the chat & cuppa
than the actual fix – o

but it's nice to be wanted
God says outloud

(mister & mrs number thirty-seven
hear the voices of the seven thunderous
pneumatic drills)
                    & God goes
scrawls on their receipt:

not finished, be back Monday

KEELY CELIA LAUFER

CHANUKAH

From the corner
between the kitchen sink
and fingering her cigarette lighter,
my gentile mother watched

my father set up his childhood
Menorah and light
at our peeling table.

He gabbled in faith
the letters of roofless houses
and I watched from the doorway

doped up on nicotined wallpaper
that had my eyes peeling candles
into cigarettes that shrank like dynamite sticks,

burning the festival of light out between days
into ash at the base of Menorah cups
where my roots lie raw and cooked.

BEATRICE III

French horns wear gold
roses carved into their heart
valves and around
their lips where the sound blooms out.

She wears herself shyly on her mother's hand
sucking the insides of her cheeks red
when held up like the largest species of gold
rose – a gold rose for a right hand.

*

French horns are curled up life lines
built to make you guess how long.

After years trying
to catch her little gold tongue,
my hand is only there
to tie the knot with our lines.

*

A weight on your hip
she's a sleeping snail
to pick up and look into –
your hand her instrument,
your body her antenna.

*

I'm given an oxygen mask
to give the gift of life to.

As I begin to breathe
her pipes recoil
into a skeleton
growing gold-boned
as I breathe in
breathe blocked
as

*

Potato-handed the horn is potato-tongued
with a potato hand in her mouth she's got to
sing through, the potato in the room
we seem to hide in our mouths.

*

She's the gold potato in the room
you watch at night, wishing you
had a fairy godmother to transform
her into a pumpkin to carry you around
as her Cinderella, hold you back
once upon a time.

ŁÓDŹ
FOR MARTA AND MARIUSZ

You look the part
in your grandfather's city,

nourishing your genes with garlic,
onion, herring, kabanos,

until you ask for chips
with pancakes and orange

sorbet on top - the waitress
checks her English in Polish.

*

You sneak a sausage back
in an empty Pringles tin,

get busted on the British side
and asked for your Polish identity card.

RUSSIAN BEETROOT

We're introduced to Russian Jane Doe,
Zhanna Doeva

yellow of ribbed straw,
who must be dressed in your old winter clothes

must look like you this whole year at once
when teaching us how to exit an old year,

and we're instructed to draw our faces on cloth
to be strapped to Zhanna Doeva, cloth for her

to have cerise puddles for cheeks, but tonight
Zhanna Doeva can only have one of our faces,

and those too lost not to stare at her
will have their tunnel vision cooled with beetroot

rubbed into our cheeks by coach Elena,
now me and the kids look like Zhanna Doeva

and I'm lucky to be the only adult painted
with the tea towel of embarrassment

so I can be pink under red and burn
my embarrassment paint sticky,

and no one will know I'm embarrassed when asked
if beetroot-faced boy I'm with is my husband

– he's by me and he's red – he's kicking the log
in the game where we push each other

to push the log over and he's pulling the hat
from the other man's head as the game says,

and he's touching the nose then the ankle
of the women next to him in the circle while it moves,

because the little girl in the middle is in charge
and tells us all to and he whispers 'fuck,

what is this? The Russians are crazy. I can't believe
you invited me' and I say 'Shhh',

and we watch Zhanna Doeva being pushed
down the stairs, being greeted with a stare

then a clap at the bottom, and bliny is brought out,
they stand for the Sun, hot and skin-coloured

in need of dried beetroot on top to cover the embarr
assment we're chewing between our voices,

and Galina offers me dried beetroot flakes
from her hand like I'm a cat who knows the hand

of Russian culture, I say 'Spasiba', but he pauses
to sniff it first in his head and I mumble 'koshka'

and he says 'kosha' and she says to the boy,
'Is she your partner?'

and I eat each flake of embarrassment
off of the face of the sun

wishing Zhanna Doeva had taken my own –
he doesn't know he's just called me 'babe' in Russian –

'Do you like it' the boy says smiling, 'it tastes nice' I say,
'here you are taste it'. He likes it and we share

something red inside that he thinks is Russian
but it's just beetroot, the celebration of embarrassment

called Maslenitsa, where you scare the year's
embarrassment out with beetroot and sun,

and sit on the tube, look into the glass and realise –
I'm dyed with embarrassment, and he doesn't tell me,

maybe he thought he wasn't ready, I smell earthy –
I smell earthy, I smell earthy on the tube

and everyone coming and going is staring,
and we look straight past faces, straining

embarrassment from our cheeks, pretending
we're Zhanna Doeva and only leave the house yearly.

ELIZABETH LEWIS WILLIAMS

*

THE PRACTICAL APPLICATION
OF IONOSPHERICS

BASE A (LOCKROY)

The blizzard sounds on glass like
streaming sand, a spitting rage
which rushes round
                    and over,

                          hits the ground

                                and runs.

Inside he's hunkered down and tuning in.

As if to coax
a signal from the needle's flicker,

his fingers turn.

CALLING THE ANTARCTICI

THE BRITISH BROADCASTING CORPORATION

28th May 1959

Dear Mrs. Lewis,

> She smoothes her coat, checks the mirror,
> *Margaret?*

In March,

> traces age lines on her face. Picks a hat.

explaining our plans for a series
of weekly broadcasts

> Still complements her eyes.
> *Are you ready?*

an invitation from the BBC

> *Margaret?*

"Calling the Antarctic"

> For a second time, she clips the letter
> (proposing coffee) and amended script

local news does lend colour and interest

into a neat black bag, just right for London,

the time allotted to each family group
is two minutes,

We don't want to miss the
train.

on Sunday, 28th June!

breathes in deeply, out again, joins
her husband at the door
her daughters at the station,
and at Bush House, Strand, WC2,

11 a.m.(our time)

will record a message to her son.

Hello, George, this is

I

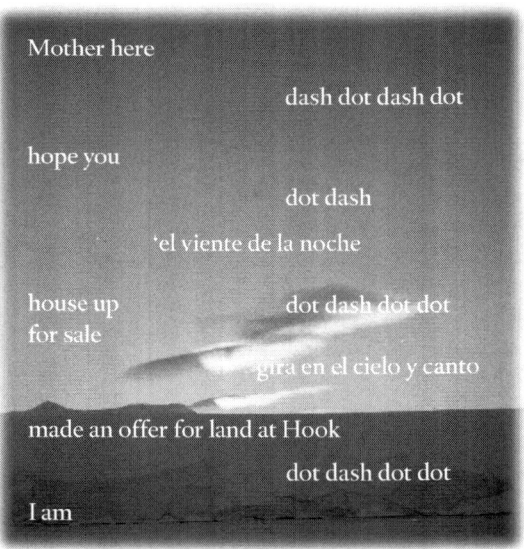

Mother here

                    dash dot dash dot

hope you

                  dot dash

        'el viente de la noche

house up   dot dash dot dot
for sale

              gira en el cielo y canto

made an offer for land at Hook

                  dot dash dot dot

I am

Flying somewhere. Already flown?
No amount of playing back could make it tell.

28TH MARCH 1959:
BEASTIE[11] AND THE TIMER UP
THE SHOOT NOBODY HAS THE
CORRECT TIME

People are required to man the machine.

Radio waves in pulses sound the universe:
their journeys timed
show distance through delay –
figures plotted on graphs, photographic traces
record the movements
of the upper atmosphere.

Like Eudoxus
constructing a model of concentric
rings he describes the layers:
troposphere, ionosphere (F1, F2, D and E)

> *When there isn't a sun to irradiate, there isn't*
> *an ionosphere (as such)*
>   *off which*
> *they can transmit our messages.*

11

He strains to hear through crackle and drift
familiar voices   10,000 miles away.

speaking to you from Plymouth
                this year   dot dot

new position going well

                    no se entienden

this week is worst.

2ND NOVEMBER 1959:
GEORGE KEEPS HAVING
HALLUCINATIONS IN THE FORM
OF STRANGE WHISTLES

over the rain drips shingle
spatter curves a fall of sound
whistlers[III] stream
along the contour lines
of earth's magnetic fields

received, transformed, transmitted
a dawn chorus with no birds
wagon wheels without a carriage
songs of auroral space

and deep in some desert sands
perhaps
the radiation of a billion joules
fuses into roots of hollowed glass
a thousand thousand flakes
of silicon or quartz

III

dash dot

met an extremely nice

dash dash dot

en absoluto

he refused to marry me before

Why bloody bother?

He has a gun above his bed Lee Enfield
.303 and an invitation to a policeman's
ball instead of a firearms certificate he's a
good shot *a murderer* according to some
last week their husky died fell off the cliff
into the water through a crack while try-
ing to dig out refuse buried in the ice he
opposed the dog not on a span and see
what happened the sun has gone behind
the glacier now and won't be seen for

some months yet instead of *sitting on his
lazy arse and cultivating a paunch* he's dig-
ging a tunnel down and then along *no one
to argue with no bloody radio or jazz* serves
no useful purpose save exercise

                               and insight into ice.

IONOGRAM

The music of the spheres, still not audible,
is here recorded on the trace
as a wave of white, its sea-spume flying
like windblown snow, or wisps of cirrus
on a matte black ground.

IV

The ionosphere excelled itself today

BASE Z (HALLEY)

There is an invisible geometry in the movement of air,
a harmony materialised in snow.

Compacted footsteps form pedestals and drifts.

Take this hut –
blown snow accumulates at a distance
before blizzards fill the space between
and bury it
fifteen foot below –
thus
all outside doors must open inwards.

In artificial light
men listen through white noise on the radio,
in a stove's warming, a needle's swing.

As the snow deepens,
a hatch in the roof is extended
upwards;

you can climb a ladder
into the sky.

I. *Calling the Antarctic* was a programme started in 1955 and recorded by the BBC for those members of the Falkland Islands Dependency Service who were overwintering in the Antarctic. A personal message of two minutes in length was recorded by family members and broadcast to a different man each week.

II. *Beastie* was the name given to the machine which was used to transmit radio waves into the upper atmosphere.

III. *Whistlers* are very low frequency electromagnetic waves generated by lightning; 'dawn chorus' and 'waggon wheels' are two names given to the different falling tones.

The black and white photographs are reproduced courtesy of the British Antarctic Survey Archives Service.
[ref. 2010/109. Copyright NERC-BAS]

ROSIE QUATTROMINI

ESSAY
(A POEM FOR JENNY DISKI)

if this is what there is
then what is it like?

what is it like to be
mirroring the abyss
like this?

as we move from quotation
to indirect statement
we gain distance and yet
can it be objective?

as we incite these blank spaces
distance can grow between
these atomic bodies;
we cannot create much
together but we can create a negative

nonetheless grasping the image
of the phantom of life we
traverse this brief period
in cradles; eternities of
darkness ahead and behind

and yet we happen to cross
in this brief crack of light

st ambrose was the first person
to read without moving his lips
but still he followed the words
with his finger; flesh against ink

on paper, his heart seeking and
finding the meaning from signs
and not from sounds

now imagine
seeing ambrose
through the window

as he reads

as he thinks

as he learns

as he enters into
a contract with the text
and attempts through the act
of silent reading
to construct the
subjective experience
of another
within his own
subjective experience
of the world;
what a piece of work
is man, to cram
the whole universe
into such scant space

can you choose between
thinking and living?
would you?

swung in a cradle that looks
like a coffin, the infant contemplates
its existence; would it prefer
to have been born a bat?

marie takes sixteen paces towards
the unbound volume; 'opinion
changes', but the devotion of
the intellect remains constant

she feels that sharpness slice into
the flesh of many forearms
spanning history with their reach

it becomes difficult to function;
it is difficult to function without
rules: in language it is impossible

still we attempt, we try, we try
to never finish, to edit
to never finish
to digress

put simply

you taught me a lot

and

i miss you

i can talk around it but
that is what i really want to say

how did we think without
language?

close the gap

language is an abstraction
we must take back to the sign
destroy the blank space
cross it out
destroy the abyss
make connections between
eternities; make the pre and post
the synchronous now
make concrete image
make positive

if this is what there is
then what is it like?

it is like this, and this is what we do.

NOCTURNE

it is 4am
now i shall lay my body down
now i shall sleep for 12 hours
now i shall dream of supermarkets
self-service checkouts
train ticket dispensers
bodies rising from their graves
spitting out their metal tongues
beginning anew in pallor and frigidity
a world order of abstinence
(o do not touch me for my spirit is weak
and my flesh is willing
but my spirit will wake tomorrow
and feel sad)

in this dream my eyeballs are square
i do not know if anyone else's are

there is a scuttling thing in the air
wingbeats or claws i cannot tell

in my dream i cannot sleep

THERE IS ONLY ONE
VERSION OF THIS MOMENT
AND THEN IT IS GONE

time wasting is a method
for avoiding potential
pain but

everyone i know is getting engaged
getting a house moving to london
living with love and growing
up and out and expanding
into the world while i sit

here

a shell of a hazelnut so tiny
that i can fit neatly into
the palm of an anchorite's hand:

i contain multitudes
but then again we all do
it's nothing much really.

SEAN WAI KEUNG

STEALING TABLE SAUCES
FROM WETHERSPOONS

at lunch   you tell me you miss going to church
                              the rituals   the something
                              to fill up the lack

i am eyeing up
the sauce basket
beside you

its not enough
                              you say
                                        this
                                        isnt
                                        enough

after lunch my pockets are bulging
with colmans mustard/hp/cholula
hot in the rain you tell me   im a bad human being
                    you ask me why

i try to explain the comfort of it
the complete relief of having a fridge
filled up a shelf perfectly lined
the safe knowledge that with enough
condiments any meal is edible

                    you say   but what about
                                        their business models

i tell you not to worry
this happens all the time

anything they lose
they can always simply replace

THE SEA IS GREY + EVEN

though we arent kids

we go under the pier

looking for a makeout

spot + it starts to rain

+ theres slippery wet

seaweed blending into

sand everywhere + as

we press close to each

other that sea sound

forms a *whsh* _____ *whsh*____*whsh*_____ *whsh*

kind of rhythm + huge

birds squawk + the crazy golf place is shut + the
        whsh _____ *whsh*____*whsh*_____ *whsh*
   amusement park

above us on the pier is shut + the wind is crazy

strong so very fucking strong so strong its   crazy
     whsh _____ *whsh*____*whsh*_____ *whsh*
to think that the birds
  whsh _____ *whsh*____*whsh*_____ *whsh*
are still strong enough

to fly through but they
     whsh _____ *whsh*____*whsh*_____ *whsh*
do + seeing that strength
  whsh _____ *whsh*____*whsh*_____ *whsh*

really inspires me + in
                        whsh _____ *whsh*____*whsh*_____ *whsh*

that moment i never *whsh* _____ *whsh*____*whsh*_____ *whsh*

want us to be any *whsh*____*whsh*_____ *whsh*

where else but *whsh* _____ *whsh*____*whsh*_____ *whsh*
                   whsh _____ *whsh*____*whsh*_____ *whsh*

        whsh _____ *whsh*____*whsh*_____ *whsh*
    whsh _____ *whsh*____*whsh*_____ *whsh*

  whsh _____ *whsh*____*whsh*_____ *whsh*
                 here

     whsh _____ *whsh*____*whsh*_____ *whsh*

       whsh _____ *whsh*____*whsh*_____ *whsh*

         whsh _____ *whsh*____*whsh*_____ *whsh*

I AM ON THE FLOOR CUTTING
ROAST DUCK INTO BITS

the portrait on the kitchen wall is slanted

there are three plug sockets – kettle – microwave
– electric incense
only one is being used

sometimes i wish i was catholic
– gold+white is a better aesthetic
than red+brown

from the other room
麻將 is being played
everyone is yelling

i get shouted at
to focus on cutting   each duckbit equally

except the offerings –
they have to be smaller

but i dont know how small

just three little pieces

from the body

i have yet to figure out how best to structure
each of my prayers into language

CYCLING AT NIGHT
WITH NO LIGHTS

as a child three things scared me most
>   * being alone in the dark
>   * being hit by an ambulance
>   * being one of those male poets who says things
>   like its so lovely when girls wear short skirts on
>   their bikes

but this is progress

>   * somewhere ahead of me she weaves
>   between street lights + traffic + i worry
>   about her falling + breaking her legs + dying
>   in an entanglement of mechanics + short skirt

>   * above me the moon is as huge as an ego
>   an ambulance speeds past + i think for a moment
>   that its coming for me + when i realise its not
>   i feel relief but also fear

>   * i realise then that no matter how hard i try
>   im not as strong as she is
>   + im already almost out of breath
>   – i may never be able   to catch up

but i will keep going

BIOGRAPHIES

AL ANDERSON is a British poet and dramatist. His work concerns queerness, lyric identity, memory and the poetics of 'looking', and was recently translated into Italian and published in the Rome-based journal *Rapso X*. He lives and works in South East London.

MEGHANN BOLTZ is from Buffalo, New York. She holds an MA in Comparative Literature from Goldsmiths, University of London.

ELEANOR CHANDLER grew up in Sydney. She lives in London and works at *Granta* magazine. Her work can be found in *Textual Practice*, the *Suburban Review*, *Elbow Room*, *For Every Year*, the *Bohemyth* and *Seizure*. You can tweet her @eleanorchandler.

GEORGIA HINGSTON writes poems to help alleviate the anxiety of existing. She is a prose poem enthusiast and has participated in the Enemies Project and performed at Noted Festival 2016.

JOANNA HOLLINS writes about family, theology, growing up in Milton Keynes, and bees. She has previously been published in the UEA undergraduate anthologies *Underworld* and *Undergrowth*, and in *Cadaverine Magazine*. She is the recipient of the Ink, Sweat and Tears Scholarship for 2015/16. More of her writing can be found at: joannahollins.wordpress.com.

KEELY CELIA LAUFER is the recipient of The UEA Literary Festival Poetry Scholarship 2015/16. She interviews and reviews for *Poetry Wales* magazine and has had poetry published in *The Lampeter Review*, issue 11, and forthcoming in *Cheval 9* anthology by Parthian Books. Her first journal article, 'The language of teeth: the tooth as a physical embodiment of identity in literature', has recently been published in *New Writing: The International Journal for the Practice and Theory of Creative Writing* with Taylor & Francis/Routledge. She is also a French horn and trumpet player and studies Russian. @KeelyCelia.

ELIZABETH LEWIS WILLIAMS is a Norwich-based poet and teacher. This sequence is part of a collection based on her father's time in the Antarctic. Published in *The Fenland Reed*, *The Red Wheelbarrow* and *Lighthouse*, a selection of her work can also be found at: elw0168@wordpress.com.

ROSIE QUATTROMINI is originally from Norwich. She read English at Queens' College, Cambridge before coming to UEA, and her academic areas of interest include Renaissance poetics, Latin literature, Gothic, avant-garde theatre, and surrealism. You can find her @RosieThinksThis.

SEAN WAI KEUNG is interested in poetry and performance. He was awarded the 2013 Farrago Zoo Award for 'Best Debut Performance' and the 2016 'Funniest Poem' prize for the Café Writers Open Poetry Competition. He regularly organises poetry and performance events across the country. Follow him at: jellyfisharepoemstoo.tumblr.com.

ACKNOWLEDGEMENTS

Thanks are due to the School of Literature, Drama and Creative Writing at UEA in partnership with Egg Box Publishing for making the UEA MA Creative Writing anthologies possible.

We'd also like to thank the following people:

Trezza Azzopardi, Tiffany Atkinson, Andrew Cowan, Giles Foden, Vesna Goldsworthy, Sarah Gooderson, Rachel Hore, Kathryn Hughes, Sarah Jones, Catrina Laskey, Timothy Lawrence, Jean McNeil, Jeremy Noel-Tod, Beatrice Poubeau, Denise Riley, Sophie Robinson, Kathy Scales, Helen Smith, Henry Sutton, Ian Thomson, Steve Waters, Peter Womack

Nathan Hamilton at Egg Box Publishing, Thom Swann and Ray O'Meara of A New Archive and Daniel Frost.

Editorial team:
Katherine Allen
Justine Ashford
Meghann Boltz
Sally Fox
Patrick Hughes
Rashmee Roshan Lall
Keely Celia Laufer
James McDermott
Lucy Malouf
Richard O'Halloran
Arron Westbrook
J Y Yang

COLOPHON

UEA Creative Writing MA Anthology:
Poetry, 2016

International © 2016 retained by individual authors

A CIP record for this book is available from the
British Library.

Designed by A New Archive.

Cover illustration by Daniel Frost.

Proofread by Sarah Gooderson.

Printed and bound in the UK by TJ International.

Distributed by
NBN International,
10 Thornbury Road
Plymouth PL6 7PP
t. +44 (0)1752 2023102
e. cservs@nbninternational.com

ISBN: 978-1911343127